Facts About the Red Panda

By Lisa Strattin

© 2019 Lisa Strattin

FREE BOOK

FREE FOR ALL SUBSCRIBERS

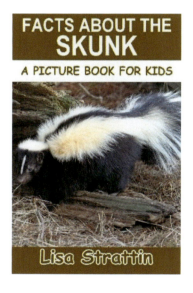

LisaStrattin.com/Subscribe-Here

BOX SET

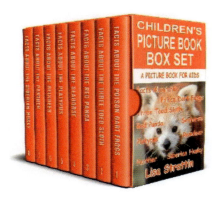

- **FACTS ABOUT THE POISON DART FROGS**
- **FACTS ABOUT THE THREE TOED SLOTH**
- **FACTS ABOUT THE RED PANDA**
- **FACTS ABOUT THE SEAHORSE**
- **FACTS ABOUT THE PLATYPUS**
- **FACTS ABOUT THE REINDEER**
- **FACTS ABOUT THE PANTHER**
- **FACTS ABOUT THE SIBERIAN HUSKY**

LisaStrattin.com/BookBundle

Facts for Kids Picture Books by Lisa Strattin

Little Blue Penguin, Vol 92

Chipmunk, Vol 5

Frilled Lizard, Vol 39

Blue and Gold Macaw, Vol 13

Poison Dart Frogs, Vol 50

Blue Tarantula, Vol 115

African Elephants, Vol 8

Amur Leopard, Vol 89

Sabre Tooth Tiger, Vol 167

Baboon, Vol 174

Sign Up for New Release Emails Here

LisaStrattin.com/subscribe-here

All rights reserved. No part of this book may be reproduced by any means whatsoever without the written permission from the author, except brief portions quoted for purpose of review.

All information in this book has been carefully researched and checked for factual accuracy. However, the author and publisher makes no warranty, express or implied, that the information contained herein is appropriate for every individual, situation or purpose and assume no responsibility for errors or omissions. The reader assumes the risk and full responsibility for all actions, and the author will not be held responsible for any loss or damage, whether consequential, incidental, special or otherwise, that may result from the information presented in this book.

All images are free for use or purchased from stock photo sites or royalty free for commercial use.

Some coloring pages might be of the general species due to lack of available images.

I have relied on my own observations as well as many different sources for this book and I have done my best to check facts and give credit where it is due. In the event that any material is used without proper permission, please contact me so that the oversight can be corrected.

COVER IMAGE

https://flickr.com/photos/benoitdupont/5759595404/

**ADDITIONAL IMAGES*

https://flickr.com/photos/sadiehart/7613217648/

https://flickr.com/photos/a-m-lewis/5177155314/

https://flickr.com/photos/kuribo/2162316640/

https://flickr.com/photos/7718908@N04/6545372265/

https://flickr.com/photos/watts_photos/26795765640/

https://flickr.com/photos/benoitdupont/5759053231/

https://flickr.com/photos/mndapnda421/4441744445/

https://flickr.com/photos/flamesworddragon/8308341584/

https://flickr.com/photos/9557815@N05/3739160644/

https://flickr.com/photos/_pavan_/27725425196/

Contents

INTRODUCTION..9

CHARACTERISTICS 11

APPEARANCE 13

LIFE STAGES 15

LIFE SPAN 17

SIZE 19

HABITAT... 21

DIET 23

ENEMIES.. 25

SUITABILITY AS PETS... 27

INTRODUCTION

The Red Panda is a cat-sized meat eating mammal found living in the temperate mountain forests on the slopes of the Himalayas. They are related to the larger and more famous Giant Panda, although the exact closeness of their relationship remains uncertain to science. They also share a number of characteristics with the Raccoon, so Red Pandas are classified in a family all their own.

The Red Panda is also known by a number of other names in their native regions: the Lesser Panda, the Red Cat-Bear, and as the Fire Fox in Nepal. Just like the Giant Panda, the Red Panda eats bamboo and with rapid deforestation of these unique areas there is less for these animals to eat as time progresses, which has ultimately caused the Red Panda to be listed as an endangered species.

CHARACTERISTICS

The Red Panda is a nocturnal animal and is usually solitary animal, except during mating season. They spend the day time sleeping in branches high in the tree canopy where they live, with their long, bushy tail wrapped around them to keep them warm.

Although they have been known to eat in the trees, they usually come down to the ground after dusk and begin foraging in the safety of the darkness. They are a territorial animal that marks their home area with droppings, and urine. They communicate with one another using short whistles and squeaks. They are strong and agile climbers that can sleep safely in the branches during the day but also can dart up a trunk if threatened by predators using their sharp claws to hang on.

Living high in the cold mountain climate means that they are well suited to staying warm with their dense fur and bushy, blanket-like tail. However, on really cold days they have been known to sunbathe high in the treetops to warm themselves up while they are sleeping during the day.

APPEARANCE

The Red Panda is about the same size as a large housecat, with a cute, cat-like face and a long, bushy tail. They have rusty colored thick fur that covers their body except for their whitish colored ears, cheeks, muzzle and spots above their eyes. They also have reddish-brown stripes that run down either side of their white muzzle, as well as the alternating light and dark rings all up and down their tails.

The Red Panda has semi-retractable claws that help in climbing and provide stability on the branches and strong, tough jaws which are needed to chew on bamboo. Like the Giant Panda, the Red Panda has an extended wrist bone which acts a bit like your thumb This allows them to hold onto bamboo while chewing on it.

LIFE STAGES

Red Pandas usually breed between January and March and after a gestation period of about four months, the female gives birth to 1 to 5 cubs. The cubs are born blind and although they begin to open their eyes within a couple of weeks, the eyes of the cubs don't fully open until they are about a month old.

Before her cubs are born, the female builds a nest in a tree-hole, roots or a bamboo thicket which she has lined with leaves, moss and other soft plant matter. The cubs may not leave the nest until they are three months of age and are strong enough to negotiate the tricky branches. They feed solely on bamboo until they are old enough to digest other foods, and then reach their full adult size after about a year.

LIFE SPAN

Red Pandas live for 8 to 12 years.

SIZE

Most adult Red Pandas are between 2 and 4 feet long and weigh 7 to 14 pounds.

HABITAT

The Red Panda is found living in the Himalayas at altitudes of between 6,000 and 13,000 feet. The high mountain slopes are usually covered in deciduous hardwood forest with a bamboo underlayer that is needed for the Red Panda's survival.

Due to the fragile ecology of their native forest, the Red Panda is being pushed into smaller and more isolated areas of their once very wide home range because of the lack of significant amounts of bamboo for them to eat.

DIET

Although the Red Panda belongs to the meat eating group of mammals, their diet is significantly vegetarian because bamboo shoots make up the majority of their food.

Unlike the Giant Panda, the Red Panda will also eat a variety of other foods to supplement its diet, like acorns, berries and grasses, as well as grubs, mice, lizards, chicks and birds' eggs.

Along with excellent sight, smell and hearing, the Red Panda also has long, white whiskers on its snout which help it to move through the dense vegetation in the dark of night, when it is searching for food.

ENEMIES

Due to the fact that Red Pandas live in high-altitude mountain forests, they actually have fewer natural predators than they would have if they lived further down. Snow Leopards and Martens are the only real predators of the Red Panda along with Birds of Prey and small carnivores that prey on the more vulnerable cubs

SUITABILITY AS PETS

Red Pandas have been admired by people for years but many of the experiences that we have with them are in zoo. They are generally difficult to spot in the wild, since they are out mostly at night. They are not a good choice for a pet, and if you want to see them, you might be able to see them in your local zoo.

COLOR ME

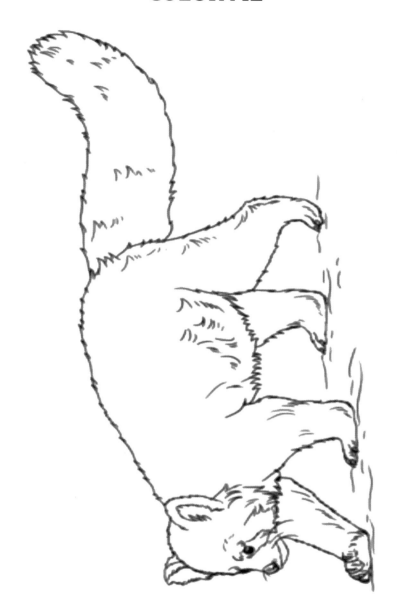

COLOR ME

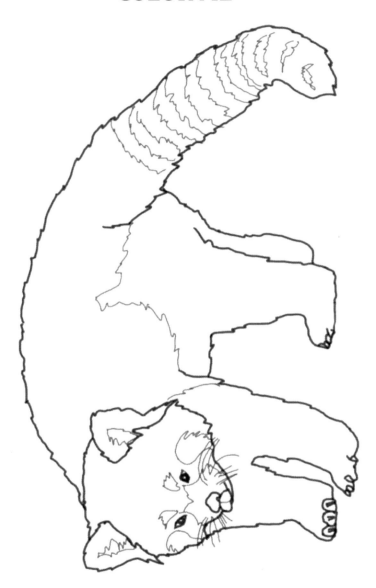

COLOR ME

COLOR ME

COLOR ME

COLOR ME

COLOR ME

COLOR ME

COLOR ME

COLOR ME

Please leave me a review here:

LisaStrattin.com/Review-Vol-205

For more Kindle Downloads Visit Lisa Strattin Author Page on Amazon Author Central

amazon.com/author/lisastrattin

To see upcoming titles, visit my website at LisaStrattin.com– most books available on Kindle!

LisaStrattin.com

FREE BOOK

FOR ALL SUBSCRIBERS – SIGN UP NOW

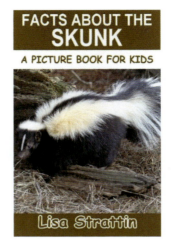

LisaStrattin.com/Subscribe-Here

LisaStrattin.com/Facebook

LisaStrattin.com/Youtube

Printed in Great Britain
by Amazon